Belgium

by

Joseph E. Morris

Double9 BOOKS

Belgium

by Joseph E. Morris

ISBN: 978-93-74836-39-2

Published by

DOUBLE 9 BOOKS
2/13-B, Ansari Road
Daryaganj, New Delhi – 110002
info@double9books.com
www.double9books.com
Tel. 011-40042856

ABOUT THE AUTHOR

Joseph E. Morris was an English author and travel writer known for his concise yet insightful guidebooks that explored various regions of Europe during the late 19th and early 20th centuries. His works often combined geographical detail with cultural and historical reflection, making them valuable companions for travellers of his time. Morris's writings, particularly those focused on European countries such as Belgium, France, and Italy, highlighted his appreciation for architecture, art, and the everyday life of people within diverse landscapes. He had a gift for portraying cities not merely as physical spaces but as living embodiments of historical continuity and cultural identity. Through his travel accounts, Morris contributed to an early form of literary tourism, encouraging readers to observe foreign lands with curiosity and respect. His clear prose, supported by historical accuracy and artistic sensitivity, reflected a broader humanistic outlook. Although little biographical detail is available about his personal life, his work remains recognized for its clarity, accessibility, and enduring contribution to cultural geography and travel literature.

CONTENTS

CHAPTER I

It needs, indeed, an effort of the imagination at the moment of writing to think of Belgium as in any sense a component part of "Beautiful Europe." The unhappy "cockpit" of the Continent at the actual hour is again in process of accomplishing its frightful destiny—no treaty, or "scrap of paper," is potent to preserve this last, and weakest, of all the nations of Western Europe from drinking to the dregs the cup of ruin and desolation. Tragic indeed in the profoundest sense—in the sense of Aristotle—more tragic than the long ruin of the predestined house of Oedipus—is this accumulated tragedy of a small and helpless people, whose sole apparent crime is their stern determination to cling at any cost to their plighted word of honour. I have been lately glancing into a little book published about five years ago, in which a view is taken of the Belgian character that no one could term indulgent. "It is curious," says the writer in one place, "how few Belgians, old or young, rich or poor, consider the feelings or convenience of others. They are intensely selfish, and this is doubtless caused by the way in which they are brought up." And, again, in another chapter, he insinuates a doubt as to whether the Belgians, if ever called on, would even prove good soldiers. "But whether the people of a neutral State are ever likely to be brave and self-sacrificing is another thing." Such a writer certainly does not shrink—as Burke, we know, once shrank—from framing an indictment against an entire people. Whether Belgium, as a nation, is self-sacrificing and brave may safely be left to the judgment of posterity. There is a passage in one of Mr. Lecky's books—I cannot put my finger on the exact reference—in which he pronounces that the sins of France, which are many, are forgiven her, because, like the woman in the Gospels, she has loved much. It is not our business now, if indeed at any time, to appraise the sins of Belgium; but surely her love, in anguish, is manifest and supreme. When we contemplate these firstfruits of German "kultur"—this deluge of innocent blood, and this wreckage of ancient monuments—who can hesitate for a moment to belaud this little people, which has flung itself thus gallantly, in the spirit of purest sacrifice, in front of the onward progress of this new and frightful Juggernaut? Rather one recalls that old persistent creed, exemplified perhaps in the mysteries, now of the Greek Adonis, now of Persian Mithras, and now of the Roman priest of the Nennian lake, that it is only through the gates of sacrifice and death that the world moves on triumphant to rejuvenation and life. Is it, in truth, through the blood of a bruised and prostrate Belgium that the purple hyacinth of a rescued European civilization will spring presently from the soaked and untilled soil?

Yet even if German "kultur" in the end sweep wholly into ruin the long accumulated treasures of Belgian architecture, sculpture, and painting—if Bruges, which to-day stands still intact, shall to-morrow be reckoned with Dinant and Louvain—yet it would still be worth while to set before a few more people this record of vanished splendour, that they may better appreciate what the world has lost through lust of brutal ambition, and better be on guard in the future to protect what wreckage is left. All these treasures were bequeathed to us—not to Belgium alone, but to the whole world—by the diligence and zeal of antiquity; and we have seen this goodly heritage ground in a moment into dust beneath the heel of an insolent and degraded militancy. Belgium, in very truth, in guarding the civilization and inheritance of other nations, has lavishly wrecked her own. "They made me keeper of the vineyards; but my own vineyard have I not kept."

Luckily, however, it is not yet quite clear that the "work of waste and ruin" is wholly irreparable. One sees in the illustrated English papers pictures of the great thirteenth-century churches at Dixmude, Dinant, and Louvain, made evidently from photographs, that suggest at least that it is not impossible still to rebuild the walls of Jerusalem. Dixmude, indeed—I judge from an interior view—is possibly shattered past hope; but Dinant and St. Pierre, at Louvain, so far at least as their fabrics are concerned, seem to lack little but the woodwork of their roofs. It is only a few years ago since the writer stood in the burnt-out shell of Selby Abbey; yet the Selby Abbey of to-day, though some ancient fittings of inestimable value have irreparably perished, is in some ways not less magnificent, and is certainly more complete, than its imperfect predecessor. One takes comfort, again, in the thought of York Minster in the conflagration caused by the single madman Martin in 1829, and of the collapse of the blazing ceilings in nave and chancel, whilst the great gallery of painted glass, by some odd miracle, escaped. Is it too much to hope that this devil's work of a million madmen at Dixmude or Nieuport may prove equally incomplete?

In the imperfect sketch that follows I write of the aspect of Belgium—of its cities, that were formerly the most picturesque in Europe; of its landscapes, that range from the level fens of Flanders to the wooded limestone wolds of the Ardennes—as I knew these, and loved them, in former years, before hell was let loose in Europe. And perhaps, the picture here presented will in time be not altogether misrepresentative of the regenerated Belgium that will certainly some day arise.

CHAPTER II

It is not merely in its quality of unredeemed and absolute flatness that the great fen country of Flanders is so strongly reminiscent of the great fen country of the Holland parts of Lincolnshire. Each of these vast levels is equally distinguished by the splendour and conspicuousness of its ancient churches. Travelling by railway between Nieuport and Dixmude, you have on every side of you, if the day be clear, a prospect of innumerable towers and spires, just as you have if you travel by railway between Spalding and Sleaford, or between Spalding and King's Lynn. The difference, perhaps, is that the Lincolnshire churches present finer architectural feature, and are built of stone, floated down in barges, by dyke or fen, from the famous inland quarries of Barnack, in Northamptonshire; whilst most of those in Flanders are built of local brick, though the drums of the piers and the arches are often of blue limestone. It is remarkable, certainly, that these soaring spires should thus chiefly rise to eminence in a setting of dead, flat plain. It may well be, indeed, as some have suggested, that the character of architecture is unconsciously determined by the type of surrounding scenery; that men do not build spires in the midst of mountains to compete with natural sublimity that they cannot hope to emulate, but are emboldened to express in stone and mortar their own heavenward aspirations in countries where Nature seems to express herself in less spiritual, or at any rate in less ambitious, mood.

As we cross the level prairie between these two little towns of West Flanders (we hope to visit them presently), a group of lofty roofs and towers is seen grandly towards the west, dominating the fenland with hardly less insistency than Boston "Stump," in Lincolnshire, as seen across Wash and fen. This is the little town of Furnes, than which one can hardly imagine a quainter place in Belgium, or one more entirely fitted as a doorway by which to enter a new land. Coming straight from England by way of Calais and Dunkirk, the first sight of this ancient Flemish market-place, with its unbroken lines of old white-brick houses, many of which have crow-stepped gables; with the two great churches of St. Nicholas, with its huge square tower, and of St. Walburge, with its long ridge of lofty roof; and with its Hotel de Ville and Palais de Justice of about the dawn of the seventeenth century, is a revelation, in its atmosphere of sleepy evening quiet, to those who rub their eyes with wonder, and find it hard to credit that London, "with its unutterable, external hideousness," was actually left behind them only that very morning, and is actually at present not two hundred miles distant. Furnes, in short, is an epitome, and I think a very charming one, of all that is most characteristic in Flanders; and not the less charming because here the strong currents of modern life that throb through Ghent and Antwerp extend only to its threshold in the faintest of dying ripples, and because you do not need to be told that in its town hall may still be seen hangings of old Spanish leather, and that the members of the Inquisition used to meet in the ante-chamber of the first floor of its Palais de Justice, in order to throw yourself back in memory to those old days of Lowland greatness from whose struggles Holland emerged victorious, but into which Belgium, for the time, sank back oppressed.

Furnes—in Flemish Veurne—is an excellent centre from which to explore the extreme west point of Belgian Flanders, which is also the extreme west point of Belgium as a whole. Flanders, be it always remembered, does not terminate with mere, present-day, political divisions, but spreads with unbroken character to the very gateways of Calais and Lille. Hazebrouck, for example, is a thoroughly Flemish town, though nearly ten miles, in a beeline, inside the French border—Flemish not merely, like Dunkirk, in the architecture of its great brick church, but also actually Flemish in language, and in the names that one reads above its shop doors. In particular, excursions may be pleasantly made from Furnes—whose principal inn, the Noble Rose, is again a quaint relic of the sixteenth century—to the two delightful little market-towns of Dixmude and Nieuport-Ville: I write, as always, of what was recently, and of what I have seen myself; to-day they are probably heaps of smoking ruin, and sanguinary altars to German "kultur." Nieuport-Ville, so called in distinction from its dull little watering-place understudy, Nieuport-les-Bains, which lies a couple of miles to the west of it, among the sand-dunes by the mouth of the Yser, and is hardly worth a visit unless you want to bathe—Nieuport-Ville, in addition to its old yellow-brick Halles, or Cloth Hall, and its early Tour des Templiers, is remarkable for its possession of a fascinating church, the recent restoration of which has been altogether conservative and admirable. Standing here, in this rich and picturesque interior, you realize strongly the gulf in this direction between Belgium and France, in which latter country, in these days of ecclesiastical poverty, loving restoration of the kind here seen is rare, and whose often neglected village churches seldom, or never, exhibit that wealth of marble rood-screen and sculptured woodwork—of beaten brass and hammered iron—that distinguishes Belgian church interiors from perhaps all others on earth. The church has also some highly important brasses, another detail, common of course in most counties of England, that is now never, or hardly ever, found in France. Chief, perhaps, among these is the curious, circular brass—I hope it has escaped—with figures of husband, wife, and children, on a magnificently worked background, that is now suspended on the northwest pier of the central crossing. Very Belgian, too, in character is the rood-beam, with its three figures of Our Lord in Crucifixion, of the Virgin, and of St. John; and the striking Renaissance rood-screen in black and white marble, though not as fine as some that are found in other churches. Rood-screens of this exact sort are almost limited to Belgium, though there is one, now misplaced in the west end of the nave, and serving as an organ-loft, in the church of St. Gery at Cambrai—another curious link between French and Belgian Flanders. Dixmude (in Flemish Diksmuide), nine and a half miles south from Nieuport, is an altogether bigger and more important place, with a larger and more important church, of St. Nicholas, to match. My recollection of this last, on a Saturday afternoon of heavy showers towards the close of March, is one of a vast interior thronged with men and women in the usual dismal, black Flemish cloaks, kneeling in confession, or waiting patiently for their turn to confess, in preparation for the Easter Mass. Here the best feature, till lately, was the glorious Flamboyant rood-screen, recalling those at Albi and the church of Brou, in France; and remarkable in Belgium as one of the very few examples of its sort (there is, or was, another in St. Pierre, at Louvain) of so early a period, in a land where rood-screens, as a body, are generally much later in date.

It is difficult, in dealing with Flanders, to avoid a certain amount of architectural description, for architecture, after all, is the chief attraction of the country, save perhaps in Ghent and Bruges, where we have also noble pictures. Even those who do not care to study this architecture in detail will be gratified to stroll at leisure through the dim vastness of the great Flemish churches, where the eye is satisfied everywhere with the wealth of brass and iron work, and where the Belgian passion for wood-carving displays itself in lavish prodigality. Such wealth, indeed, of ecclesiastical furniture you will hardly find elsewhere in Western Europe—font covers of hammered brass, like those at Hal and Tirlemont; stalls and confessionals and pulpits, new and old, that are mere masses of sculptured wood-work; tall tabernacles for the reception of the Sacred Host, like those at Louvain and Leau, that tower towards the roof by the side of the High Altars. Most of this work, no doubt, is post-Gothic, except the splendid stalls and canopies (I wonder, do they still survive) at the church of St. Gertrude at Louvain; for Belgium presents few examples of mediaeval wood-work like the gorgeous stalls at Amiens, or like those in half a hundred churches in our own land. Much, in fact, of these splendid fittings is more or less contemporary with the noble masterpieces of Rubens and Vandyck, and belongs to the same great wave of artistic enthusiasm that swept over the Netherlands in the seventeenth century. Belgian pulpits, in particular, are probably unique, and certainly, to my knowledge, without parallel in Italy, England, or France. Sometimes they are merely adorned, like the confessionals at St. Charles, at Antwerp, and at Tirlemont, with isolated figures; but often these are grouped into some vivid dramatic scene, such as the Miraculous Draught of Fishes, at St. Andrew's, at Antwerp, or the Conversion of St. Norbert, in the cathedral at Malines. Certainly the fallen horseman in the latter, if not a little ludicrous, is a trifle out of place.

From Furnes to Ypres it is a pleasant journey across country by one of those strange steam-trams along the road, so common in Belgium and Holland, and not unknown in France, that wind at frequent intervals through village streets so narrow, that you have only to put out your hand in passing to touch the walls of houses. This is a very leisurely mode of travelling, and the halts are quite interminable in their frequency and length; but the passenger is allowed to stand on the open platform at the end of the carriage—though sometimes nearly smothered with thick, black smoke—and certainly no better method exists of exploring the short stretches of open country that lie between town and town. Belgian towns, remember, lie mostly thick on the ground—you are hardly out of Brussels before you come to Malines, and hardly out of Malines ere you sight the spire of Antwerp. In no part of Europe, perhaps, save in parts of Lancashire and Yorkshire, do you find so many big towns in so limited a space; yet the strips of country that lie between, though often intolerably dull, are (unlike the strips in Yorkshire) intensely rural in character. Belgian towns do not sprawl in endless, untidy suburbs, as Sheffield sprawls out towards Rotherham, and Bradford towards Leeds. Belgian towns, moreover—again unlike our own big cities in England—are mostly extremely handsome, and generally contrive, however big, to retain, at any rate in their heart, as at Antwerp, or in the Grande Place at Brussels, a striking air of antiquity; whilst some fairly big towns, such as Malines and Bruges, are mediaeval from end to end. This, of course, is not true of Belgian Luxembourg and the region of the Ardennes, where the population is much more sparse; where we do not stumble, about every fifteen miles or so, on some big town of historic name; and where the endless chessboard of little fields that lies, for example, between Ghent and Oudenarde, or between Malines and Louvain, is replaced by long contours of sweeping limestone wold, often covered with rolling wood.

Ypres is distinguished above all cities in Belgium by the huge size and stately magnificence of its lordly Cloth Hall, or Halles des Drapiers. So vast, indeed, is this huge building, and so flat the surrounding plain, that it is said that it is possible from the strangely isolated hill of Cassel, which lies about eighteen miles away to the west, just over the border, in France, on a really clear day—I have only climbed it myself, unluckily, in a fog of winter mist—to distinguish in a single view, by merely turning the head, the clustering spires of Laon, the white chalk cliffs of Kent, and this vast pile of building, like a ship at sea, that seems to lie at anchor in the heart of the "sounding plain." Nothing, perhaps, in Europe is so strangely significant of vanished greatness—not even Rome, with its shattered Forum, or Venice, with a hundred marble palaces—as this huge fourteenth-century building, with a facade that is four hundred and thirty-six feet long, and with its lofty central tower, that was built for the pride and need of Ypres, and as a market for the barter of its priceless linens, at a time when Ypres numbered a population of two hundred thousand souls (almost as big as Leicester at the present day), and was noisy with four thousand busy looms; whereas now it has but a beggarly total of less than seventeen thousand souls (about as big as Guildford), and is only a degree less sleepy than Malines or Bruges-la-Morte. Ypres, again, like Arras, has lent its name to commerce, if diaper be really rightly derived from the expression "linen of Ypres." The Cloth Hall fronts on to the Grande Place, and, indeed, forms virtually one side of it; and behind, in the Petite Place, is the former cathedral of St. Martin. This is another fine building, though utterly eclipsed by its huge secular rival, that was commenced in the thirteenth century, and is typically Belgian, as opposed to French, in the character of its architecture, and not least in its possession of a single great west tower. This last feature is characteristic of every big church in Belgium—one can add them up by the dozen: Bruges, Ghent, Louvain (though ruined, or never completed), Oudenarde, Malines, Mons—save Brussels, where the church of Ste. Gudule, called persistently, but wrongly, the cathedral, has the full complement of two, and Antwerp, where two were intended, though only one has been actually raised. This tower at Ypres, however, fails to illustrate—perhaps because it is earlier, and therefore in better taste—that astounding disproportion in height that is so frequently exhibited by Belgian towers, as at Malines, or in the case of the famous belfry in the market-place at Bruges, when considered with reference to the church, or town hall, below. In front of the High Altar, in the pavement, is an inconspicuous square of white stone, which marks the burial-place of Cornelius Jansen, who died of the plague, as Bishop of Ypres, in 1638. The monument, if you can call it monument, is scarcely less insignificant than the simple block, in the cemetery of Plainpalais at Geneva, that is traditionally said to mark the resting-place of Calvin. Yet Jansen, in his way, proved almost a second Calvin in his death, and menaced the Church from his grave with a second Reformation. He left behind in manuscript a book called "Augustinus," the predestinarian tenor of which was condemned finally, though nearly a century later, by Pope Clement XI., in 1713, in the Bull called Unigenitus. Jansenism, however, had struck deep its roots in France, and still survives in Holland at the present day, at Utrecht, as a sect that is small, indeed, but not altogether obscure. Jansen himself, it may be noted, was a Hollander by birth, having been born in 1585 at Akkoi in that kingdom.

If Ypres is to be praised appropriately as a still delightful old city that has managed to retain to a quite singular degree the outward aspect and charm of the Middle Ages, one feels that one has left one's self without any proper stock of epithets with which to appraise at its proper value the charm and romance of Bruges. Of late years, it is true, this world-famed capital of West Flanders has lost something of its old somnolence and peace. Malines, in certain quarters, is now much more dead-alive, and Wordsworth, who seems to have visualized Bruges in his mind as a network of deserted streets, "whence busy life hath fled," might perhaps be tempted now to apply to it the same prophetic outlook that he imagined for Pendragon Castle:

"Viewing
As in a dream her own renewing."

One hopes, indeed, that the renewing of Bruges will not proceed too zealously, even if Bruges come safely through its present hour of crisis. Perhaps there is no big city in the world—and Bruges, though it has shrunk pitiably, like Ypres, from its former great estate in the Middle Ages, has still more than forty thousand souls—that remains from end to end, in every alley, and square, and street, so wholly unspoilt and untouched by what is bad in the modern spirit, or that presents so little unloveliness and squalor in its more out-of-the-way corners as Bruges. Bruges, of course, like Venice, and half a dozen towns in Holland, is a strangely amphibious city that is intersected in every direction, though certainly less persistently than Venice, by a network of stagnant canals. On the other hand, if it never rises to the splendour of the better parts of Venice—the Piazza and the Grand Canal—and lacks absolutely that charm of infinitely varied, if somewhat faded or even shabby, colour that characterizes the "Queen of the Adriatic," there is yet certainly nothing monotonous in her monotone of mellow red-brick; and certainly nothing so dilapidated, and tattered, and altogether poverty-stricken as one stumbles against in Venice in penetrating every narrow lane, and in sailing up almost every canal. Of Venice we may perhaps say, what Byron said of Greece, that

"Hers is the loveliness in death
That parts not quite with parting breath";

whilst in Bruges we recognize gladly, not death or decay at all, but the serene and gracious comeliness of a dignified and vital old age.

We cannot, of course, attempt, in a mere superficial sketch like this, even to summarize briefly the wealth of objects of interest in Bruges, or to guide the visitor in detail through its maze of winding streets. Two great churches, no doubt, will be visited by everyone—the cathedral of St. Sauveur and the church of Notre Dame—both of which, in the usual delightful Belgian fashion, are also crowded picture-galleries of the works of great Flemish masters. The See of Bruges, however, dates only from 1559; and even after that date the Bishop had his stool in the church of St. Donatian, till this was destroyed by the foolish Revolutionaries in 1799. In a side-chapel of Notre Dame, and carefully boarded up for no reason in the world save to extort a verger's fee for their exhibition, are the splendid black marble monuments, with recumbent figures in copper gilt, of Charles the Bold, who fell at Nancy in 1477 (but lives for ever, with Louis XI. of France, in the pages of "Quentin Durward"), and of his daughter, Mary, the wife of the Emperor Maximilian, of Austria, who was killed by being thrown from her horse whilst hunting in 1482. These two tombs are of capital interest to those who are students of Belgian history, for Charles the Bold was the last male of the House of Burgundy, and it was by the marriage of his daughter that the Netherlands passed to the House of Hapsburg, and thus ultimately fell under the flail of religious persecution during the rule of her grandson, Spanish Philip. Close to Notre Dame, in the Rue St. Catherine, is the famous old Hospital of St. Jean, the red-brick walls of which rise sleepily from the dull waters of the canal, just as Queens' College, or St. John's, at Cambridge, rise from the sluggish Cam. Here is preserved the rich shrine, or chasse, "resembling a large Noah's ark," of St. Ursula, the sides of which are painted with scenes from the virgin's life by Hans Memling, who, though born in the neighbourhood of Mayence, and thus really by birth a German, lived for nearly a quarter of a century or more of his life in Bruges, and is emphatically connected, like his master Roger van der Weyden and the brothers Van Eyck, with the charming early Flemish school. There is a story that he was wounded under Charles le Temeraire on the stricken field of Nancy, and painted these gemlike pictures in return for the care and nursing that he received in the Hospital of St. Jean, but "this story," says Professor Anton Springer, "may be placed in the same category as those of Durer's malevolent spouse, and of the licentiousness of the later Dutch painters." These scenes from the life of St. Ursula are hardly less delightfully quaint than the somewhat similar series that was painted by Carpaccio for the scuola of the Saint at Venice, and that are now preserved in the Accademia. Early Flemish painting, in fact, in addition to its own peculiar charm of microscopic delicacy of finish, is hardly inferior, in contrast with the later strong realism and occasional coarseness of Rubens or Rembrandt, to the tender poetic dreaminess of the primitive Italians. Certainly these pictures, though finished to the minutest and most delicate detail, are lacking in realism actually to a degree that borders on a delicious absurdity. St. Ursula and her maidens—whether really eleven thousand or eleven—in the final scene of martyrdom await the stroke of death with the stoical placidity of a regiment of dolls. "All the faces are essentially Flemish, and some of the virgins display to great advantage the pretty national feature of the slight curl in one or in both lips." A little farther along the same street is the city Picture Gallery, with a small but admirable collection, one of the gems of which is a splendid St. Christopher, with kneeling donors, with their patron saints on either side, that was also painted by Memling in 1484, and ranks as one of his best efforts. Notice also the portrait of the Canon Van de Paelen, painted by Jan van Eyck in 1436, and representing an old churchman with a typically heavy Flemish face; and the rather unpleasant picture by Gerard David of the unjust judge Sisamnes being flayed alive by order of King Cambyses. By a turning to the right out of the Rue St. Catherine, you come to the placid Minne Water, or Lac d'Amour, not far from the shores of which is one of those curious beguinages that are characteristic of Flanders, and consist of a number of separate little houses, grouped in community, each of which is inhabited by a beguine, or less strict kind of nun. In the house of the Lady Superior is preserved the small, but very splendid, memorial brass of a former inmate, who died at about the middle of the fifteenth century.

Wander where you will in the ancient streets of Bruges, and you will not fail to discover everywhere some delightful relic of antiquity, or to stumble at every street corner on some new and charming combination of old houses, with their characteristic crow-stepped, or corbie, gables. New houses, I suppose, there must really be by scores; but these, being built with inherent good taste (whether unconscious or conscious I do not know) in the traditional style of local building, and with brick that from the first is mellow in tint and harmonizes with its setting, assimilate at once with their neighbours to right and left, and fail to offend the eye by any patchy appearance or crudeness. Hardly a single street in Bruges is thus without old-world charm; but the architectural heart of the city must be sought in its two market-places, called respectively the Grande Place and the Place du Bourg. In the former are the brick Halles, with their famous belfry towering above the structure below it, with true Belgian disregard for proportion in height. It looks, indeed, like tower piled on tower, till one is almost afraid lest the final octagon should be going to topple over! In the Place du Bourg is a less aspiring group, consisting of the Hotel de Ville, the Chapelle du Saint Sang, the Maison de l'Ancien Greffe, and the Palais de Justice—all very Flemish in character, and all, in combination, elaborately picturesque. In the Chapel of the Holy Blood is preserved the crystal cylinder that is said to enshrine certain drops of the blood of Our Saviour that were brought from the Holy Land in 1149 by Theodoric, Count of Flanders, and installed in the Romanesque chapel that he built for their reception, and the crypt of which remains, though the upper chapel has long since been rebuilt, in the fifteenth century. At certain stated times the relic is exhibited to a crowd of devotees, who file slowly past to kiss it. Some congealed blood of Our Lord is also said to be preserved, after remarkable vicissitudes of loss and recovery, in the Norman Abbey of Fecamp; and mediaeval Gloucestershire once boasted as big a treasure, which brought great concourse and popularity to the Cistercian house of Hayles. Pass beneath the archway of the Maison de l'Ancien Greffe, cross the sluggish canal, and turn sharply to the left, and follow, first the cobbled Quai des Marbriers, and afterwards its continuation, the Quai Vert. Pacing these silent promenades, which are bordered by humble cottages, you have opposite, across the water, as also from the adjacent Quai du Rosaire, grand groupings of pinnacle, tower, and gable, more delightful even, in perfection of combination and in mellow charm of colour, than those "domes and towers" of Oxford whose presence Wordsworth confessed, in a very indifferent sonnet, to overpower his "soberness of reason." "In Brussels," he says elsewhere in his journal, "the modern taste in costume, architecture, etc., has got the mastery; in Ghent there is a struggle; but in Bruges old images are still paramount, and an air of monastic life among the quiet goings-on of a thinly-peopled city is inexpressibly soothing. A pensive grace seems to be cast over all, even the very children." This estimate, after the lapse of considerably more than half a century, still, on the whole, stands good.

"In Ghent there is a struggle." Approaching Ghent, indeed, by railway from Bruges, and with our heads full of old-world romance of Philip van Artevelte, and of continually insurgent burghers (for whom Ghent was rather famous), and of how Roland, "my horse without peer," "brought good news from Ghent," one is rather shocked at first, as we circle round the suburbs, at the rows of aggressive new houses, and rather tempted to conclude that the struggle has now ended, and that modernity, as at Brussels, has won the day at Ghent. Luckily the doubt is dissipated as we quit the splendid Sud station—and Belgium, one may add in parenthesis, has some of the most palatial railway-stations in the world—and find ourselves once again enmeshed in a network of ancient thoroughfares, which, if they lack wholly the absolute quiet, and in part the architectural charm, of Bruges, yet confront us at every corner with abundance of old-world charm. I suppose the six great things to be seen in Ghent are the cathedral of St. Bavon (and in the cathedral the great picture of the "Adoration of the Lamb," by Hubert and Jan van Eyck); the churches of St. Michel, with a "Crucifixion" by Van Dyck, and St. Nicholas; the wonderful old houses on the Quai des Herbes; the splendidly soaring Belfry; and possibly the Grande Beguinage, on the outskirts of the town. The cathedral has the usual solitary west tower, as at Ely, that we have now come to associate—at Ypres and Bruges—with typical Belgian churches. The great Van Eyck is hung in a chapel on the south of the choir, and the services of the verger must be sought for its exhibition. The paintings on the shutters are merely copies by Coxie, six of the originals being in the Picture Gallery in Berlin. Their restoration to Ghent, one hopes, will form a fractional discharge of the swiftly accumulating debt that Germany owes to Belgium. The four main panels, however, are genuine work of the early fifteenth century, the reredos as a whole having been begun by Hubert, and finished by Jan van Eyck in 1432. The centre-piece is in illustration of the text in the Apocalypse (v. 12): "Worthy is the Lamb that was slain to receive power, and riches, and wisdom, and strength, and honour, and glory, and blessing." One may question, indeed, if figurative language of the kind in question can ever be successfully transferred to canvas; whether this literal lamb, on its red-damasked table, in the midst of these carefully marshalled squadrons of Apostles, Popes, and Princes, can ever quite escape a hint of something ludicrous. One may question all this, yet still admire to the full both the spirit of devotion that inspired this marvellous picture and its miracle of minute and jewel-like execution. There are scores of other good pictures in Ghent, including (not even to go outside St. Bavon's) the "Christ among the Doctors" by Francis Pourbus, into which portraits of Philip II. of Spain, the Emperor Charles V., and the infamous Duke of Alva—names of terrible import in the sixteenth-century history of the Netherlands—are introduced among the bystanders; whilst to the left of Philip is Pourbus himself, "with a greyish cap on which is inscribed Franciscus Pourbus, 1567." But it is always to the "Adoration of the Mystic Lamb" that our steps are first directed, and to which they always return.

It is hard, indeed, that necessities of space should compel us to pass so lightly over other towns in Flanders—over Courtrai, with its noble example of a fortified bridge, and with its great picture, by Van Dyck, of the "Raising of the Cross" that was stolen mysteriously a few years ago from the church of Notre Dame, but has since, like the Joconde at the Louvre, been recovered and replaced; over Oudenarde, with its two fine churches, and its small town hall that is famous for its splendour even in a country the Hotels de Ville of which are easily the most elaborate (if not always the most chaste or really beautiful) in Europe; and over certain very minor places, such as Damme, to the north-east of Bruges, whose silent, sunny streets, and half-deserted churches, seem to breathe the very spirit of Flemish mediaevalism. Of the short strip of Flemish coast, from near Knocke, past the fashionable modern bathing-places of Heyst, Blankenberghe, and Ostende, to a point beyond La Panne—from border to border it measures roughly only some forty miles, and is almost absolutely straight—I willingly say little, for it seems to me but a little thing when compared with this glorious inland wealth of architecture and painting. Recently it has developed in every direction, and is now almost continuously a thin, brilliantly scarlet line of small bungalows, villas, and lodging-houses, linked up along the front by esplanades and casinos, where only a few years ago the fenland met the sea in a chain of rolling sand-dunes that were peopled only by rabbits, and carpeted only with rushes and coarse grass. About tastes there is no disputing; and there are people, no doubt, who, for some odd reason, find this kind of aggressive modernity in some way more attractive in Belgium than in Kent. For myself, I confess, it hardly seems worth while to incur the penalty of sea-sickness merely to play golf on the ruined shore of Flanders.

CHAPTER III

Of Brussels I do not propose to say very much, because Brussels, although the brightest and gayest town in Belgium, and although retaining in its Grande Place, and in the buildings that immediately surround this last, as well as in its great church of St. Gudule (which, in spite of popular usage, is not, and never was, in the proper sense a cathedral), relics of antiquity of the very highest value and interest, yet Brussels, as a whole, is so distinctively a modern, and even cosmopolitan city, and has so much general resemblance to Paris (though its site is far more picturesque, and though the place, to my mind at least, just because it is smaller and more easily comprehensible, is a much more agreeable spot to stay in), that it seems better in a sketch that is principally devoted to what is old and nationally characteristic in Belgium to give what limited space one has to a consideration rather of towns like Louvain or Malines, in which the special Belgian flavour is not wholly overwhelmed by false and extraneous influences. St. Gudule, of course, should certainly be visited, not only for the sake of the general fabric, which, notwithstanding its possession of TWO west towers, is typically Belgian in its general character, but also for the sake of its magnificent sixteenth and seventeenth century glass, and especially for the sake of the five great windows in the Chapelle du Saint Sacrement, which illustrate in a blaze of gorgeous colour the story of how Jonathan the Jew bribed Jeanne de Louvain to steal the three Consecrated Wafers, from which oozed, when sacrilegiously stabbed by the sceptical Jew, the Sacred Blood of a world's redemption. This story is told again—or rather, perhaps, a similar story in the splendid painted glass from the church of St. Eloi that is now preserved at Rouen in the Archaeological Museum. As for the Grande Place, or original market-place of the city, which is bounded on one side by the magnificent Hotel de Ville, on the opposite side by the rather heavy, rebuilt Maison du Roi, and on the remaining two sides chiefly by the splendid old seventeenth-century Corporation Houses of the various ancient city guilds—Le Renard, the house of the silk-mercers and haberdashers; Maison Cornet, the house of the boatmen, or "batelliers"; La Louvre, the house of the archers; La Brouette, the house of the carpenters; Le Sac, the house of the printers and booksellers; the Cygne, the house of the butchers; and other houses that need not be specified at any greater length, of the tailors, painters, and brewers—this is probably the completest and most splendid example of an ancient city market-square that now remains in Europe, and absolutely without rival even in Belgium itself, though similar old guild-houses, in the same delightful Flemish fashion, may still be found (though in this case with admixture of many modern buildings) in the Grande Place at Antwerp. It was in this splendid square at Brussels that the unhappy Counts of Egmont and Horn were brutally done to death, to glut the sinister tyranny of Spanish Philip, on June 5, 1568.

Also, in addition to these two superlative antiquities, two modern buildings in Brussels, though for widely different reasons, can hardly be passed over under plea of lack of space. Crowning the highest point of the city, and towering itself towards heaven in a stupendous pile of masonry, is the enormous new Palais de Justice, probably the most imposing law courts in the world. English Law undoubtedly is housed with much greater modesty, though not without due magnificence, in the altogether humbler levels of the Strand. Also in the High Town—which is the modern quarter of Brussels, in contrast with the mediaeval Low Town, which lies in the flat below—is the Royal Museum of Ancient Paintings, which probably divides honours with the Picture Gallery at Antwerp as the finest and most representative collection of pictures of the Netherlandish school in the world. Here you may revel by the hour in a candlelight effect by Gerard Dow; in the poultry of Melchior d'Hondecoeter; in a pigsty of Paul Potter's; in landscapes by Meindert Hobbema; in a moonlight landscape of Van der Neer's; in a village scene by Jan Steen; in the gallant world of Teniers; and in the weird imaginings of Pieter Brueghel the younger. The greatest pictures in the whole collection, I suppose, are those by Rubens, though he has nothing here that is comparable for a moment with those in the Picture Gallery and Cathedral at Antwerp. Very magnificent, however, is the "Woman taken in Adultery," the "Adoration of the Magi," the "Interceder Interceded" (the Virgin, at the prayer of St. Francis d'Assisi, restrains the angry Saviour from destroying a wicked world), and the "Martyrdom of St. Livinius." This last, however—like the "Crucifixion" in the Antwerp Gallery; like Van Dyck's picture in this collection of the drunken Silenus supported by a fawn; and like Rubens' own disgusting Silenus in our National Gallery at home—illustrates unpleasantly the painful Flemish facility to condescend to details, or even whole conceptions, the realism of which is unnecessarily deliberate and coarse. Here, in this death of St. Livinius, the executioner is shown in the act of presenting to a dog with pincers the bleeding tongue that he has just cut out of the mouth of the dying priest.

Brussels itself, as already intimated, is an exceedingly pleasant city for a more or less prolonged stay; and, owing at once to the admirable system of "Rundreise" tickets that are issued by the State railways at an uncommonly low price, to the rather dubious quality of the hotels in some of the smaller towns, and to the cardinal fact that Brussels is a centre from which most of the other great cities of Belgium—Malines, Ghent, Antwerp, and Liege, not to mention smaller towns of absorbing interest, such as Mons, Namur, Hal, Tirlemont, Leau, and Soignies—may be easily visited, more or less completely, in the course of a single day—owing to all these facts many people will be glad to make this pleasant city their centre, or headquarters, for the leisurely exploration of most of Belgium, with the exception of the more distant and out-of-the-way districts of West Flanders and the Ardennes. All the places enumerated are thoroughly worth visiting, but obviously only the more important can be dealt with more than just casually here. Mons, on a hill overlooking the great coalfield of the Borinage, with its strange pyramidal spoil-heaps, is itself curiously free from the dirt and squalor of an English colliery town; and equally worth visiting for the sake of its splendid cathedral of St. Wandru, the richly polychromatic effect of whose interior, due to the conjunction of deep red-brick vaulting with the dark blue of its limestone capitals and piers, illustrates another pleasant phase of Belgian ecclesiastical architecture, as well as for the sake of a contest, almost of yesterday, that has added new and immortal laurels to the genius of British battle. Tournai, on the upper Scheldt, or Escaut, is remarkable for the heavy Romanesque nave of its cathedral, which is built of the famous local black marble, as well as for its remarkable central cluster of five great towers. Soignies (in Flemish Zirick), roughly half-way between Mons and Brussels, and probably little visited, has a sombre old abbey church, of St. Vincent Maldegaire, that was built in the twelfth century, and that is enriched inside with such a collection of splendidly carved classical woodwork—stalls, misericordes, and pulpit—as you will scarcely find elsewhere even in Belgium. The pulpit in particular is wonderful, with its life-sized girl supporters, with their graceful and lightly poised figures, and pure and lovely faces. Namur, strangely enough, has really nothing of antiquity outside the doors of its Archaeological Museum, but is worth a visit if only for the pleasure of promenading streets which, if almost wholly modern, are unusually clean and bright. Tirlemont, again, has two old churches that will not delay you long, though Notre Dame de Lac has remarkably fine confessionals of the dawn of the seventeenth century, and though the splendid brass-work of the font and baptistery lectern at St. Germains would alone be worth a visit; but Leau, for which Tirlemont is the junction, is so quaint and curious a little town, and comes so much in the guise of a pleasant discovery—since Baedeker barely mentions it—that, even apart from its perfect wealth of wood and brass work in the fine thirteenth-century church of St. Leonhard, it might anyhow be thought to justify a visit to this little visited corner of South Brabant. I do not know that the brass-work could be easily matched elsewhere: the huge standard candelabrum to the north of the altar, with its crowning Crucifixion; the lectern, with its triumphant eagle and prostrate dragon; the font, with its cover, and the holy-water stoup almost as big as a small font (in Brittany I have seen them as big as a bath); and the beautiful brass railings that surround the splendid Tabernacle that was executed in 1552 by Cornelius de Vriendt, the brother of the painter Frans Floris, and that towers high into the vaulting to a height of fifty-two feet. One realizes more completely in a quiet village church like this the breadth and intensity of the wave of artistic impulse that swept through the Lowlands in the sixteenth and seventeenth centuries than is possible in half a dozen hurried visits to a picture gallery at Antwerp or Brussels. Finally Hal, to conclude our list of minor places, has a grand fourteenth-century church, with a miracle-working Virgin, and a little red-brick town hall of characteristically picturesque aspect.

The railway journey from Brussels to Antwerp traverses a typical bit of Belgian landscape that is as flat as a pancake; and the monotony is only relieved, first by the little town of Vilvoorde, where William Tyndale was burnt at the stake on October 6, 1536, though not alive, having first been mercifully strangled, and afterwards by the single, huge, square tower of Malines (or Mechlin) Cathedral, which dominates the plain from enormous distances, like the towers of Ely or Lincoln, though not, like these last, by virtue of position on a hill, but solely by its own vast height and overwhelming massiveness. Malines, though certainly containing fewer objects of particular interest than Bruges, and though certainly on the whole a less beautiful city, strikes one as hardly less dead-and-alive, and altogether may fairly claim second place among the larger Belgian cities (it houses more than fifty thousand souls) in point of mediaeval character. The great thirteenth and fourteenth century cathedral of St. Rombaut has been the seat of an archbishopric since the sixteenth century, and is still the metropolitan church of Belgium. Externally the body, like the market-hall at Bruges, is almost entirely crushed into insignificance by the utterly disproportionate height and bulk of the huge west tower, the top of which, even in its present unfinished state (one almost hopes that it may never be finished), is actually three hundred and twenty-four feet high. Boston "Stump" is only two hundred and eighty feet to the top of the weather vane, but infinitely slimmer in proportion; whilst even Salisbury spire is only about four hundred odd feet. Immediately below the parapet is the enormous skeleton clock-face, the proportions of which are reproduced on the pavement of the market-place below. The carillons in this tower are an extravagant example of the Belgian passion for chiming bells. Once safely inside the church, and the monster tower forgotten, and we are able to admire its delicate internal proportions, and the remarkable ornament of the spandrels in the great main arcades of the choir. Unfortunately, much of this interior, like that of St. Pierre at Louvain, is smothered under half an inch of plaster; but where this has been removed in tentative patches, revealing the dark blue "drums" of the single, circular columns of the arcades, the general effect is immensely improved. One would also like to send to the scrap-heap the enormous seventeenth-century figures of the Apostles on their consoles on the piers, which form so bad a disfigurement in the nave. The treasure of the church is the great "Crucifixion" by Van Dyck, which is hung in the south transept, but generally kept covered. To see other stately pictures you must go to the church of St. Jean, where is a splendid altar triptych by Rubens, the centre panel of which is the "Adoration of the Magi"; or to the fifteenth-century structure of Notre Dame au dela de la Dyle (the clumsy title is used, I suppose, for the sake of distinction from the classical Notre Dame d'Hanswyck), where Rubens' "Miraculous Draught of Fishes" is sometimes considered the painter's masterpiece. It is not yet clear whether this noble picture has been destroyed in the recent bombardment. Even to those who care little for art, a stroll to these two old churches through the sleepy back-streets of Malines, with their white and sunny houses, can hardly fail to gratify.

If Malines is a backwater of the Middle Time, as somnolent or as dull (so some, I suppose, would call it) as the strange dead towns of the Zuyder Zee, or as Coggeshall or Thaxted in our own green Essex, Antwerp, at any rate, which lies only some fifteen miles or so to the north of it, is very much awake, and of aspect mostly modern, though not without some very curious and charming relics of antiquity embedded in the heart of much recent stone and mortar. Perhaps it will be well to visit one of these at once, taking the tram direct from the magnificent Gare de l'Est (no lesser epithet is just) to the Place Verte, which may be considered the real centre of the city; and making our way thence by a network of quieter back-streets to the Musee Plantin-Moretus, which is the goal of our immediate ambition. I bring you here at once, not merely because the place itself is quite unique and of quite exceptional interest, but because it strikes precisely that note of real antiquity that underlies the modern din and bustle of Antwerp, though apt to be obscured unless we listen needfully. Happy, indeed, was the inspiration that moved the city to buy this house from its last private possessor, Edward Moretus, in 1876. To step across this threshold is to step directly into the merchant atmosphere of the sixteenth century. The once great printing house of Plantin-Moretus was founded by the Frenchman, Christopher Plantin, who was born at St. Aventin, near Tours, in 1514, and began his business life as a book-binder at Rouen. In 1549 he removed to Antwerp, and was there innocently involved one night in a riot in the streets, which resulted in an injury that incapacitated him for his former trade, and necessitated his turning to some new employment. He now set up as printer, with remarkable success, and was a sufficiently important citizen at the date of his death, in 1589, to be buried in his own vault under a chapel in the Cathedral. The business passed, on his decease, to his son-in-law, Jean Moertorf, who had married his daughter, Martine, in 1570, and had

Latinized his surname to Moretus in accordance with the curious custom that prevailed among scholars of the sixteenth century. Thus Servetus was really Miguel Servete, and Thomas Erastus was Thomas Lieber. The foundation of the fortunes of the house was undoubtedly its monopoly—analogous to that enjoyed by the English house of Spottiswoode, and by the two elder Universities—of printing the liturgical works—Missals, Antiphons, Psalters, Breviaries, etc.—that were used throughout the Spanish dominions. No attempt, however, seems to have been made in the later stages of the history of the house to adopt improved machinery, or to reconstruct the original, antiquated buildings. The establishment, accordingly, when it was taken over by the city in 1876, retained virtually the same aspect as it had worn in the seventeenth century, and remains to the present day perhaps the best example in the world of an old-fashioned city business house of the honest time when merchant-princes were content to live above their office, instead of seeking solace in smug suburban villas. The place has been preserved exactly as it stood, and even the present attendants are correctly clad in the sober brown garb of the servants of three hundred years since. It is interesting, not only in itself, but as an excellent example of how business and high culture were successfully combined under the happier economic conditions of the seventeenth and eighteenth centuries. The Plantin-Moretus family held a high position in the civic life of Antwerp, and mixed in the intellectual and artistic society for which Antwerp was famed in the seventeenth century—the Antwerp of Rubens (though not a native) and Van Dyck, of Jordaens, of the two Teniers, of Grayer, Zegers, and Snyders. Printing, indeed, in those days was itself a fine art, and the glories of the house of Plantin-Moretus rivalled those of the later Chiswick Press, and of the goodly Chaucers edited in our own time by Professor Skeat, and printed by William Morris. Proof-reading was then an erudite profession, and Francois Ravelingen, who entered Plantin's office as proof-reader in 1564, and assisted Arias Montanus in revising the sheets of the Polyglot Bible, is said to have been a great Greek and Oriental scholar, and crowned a career of honourable toil, like Hogarth's Industrious Apprentice, by marrying his master's eldest daughter, Marguerite, in 1565. The room in which these scholars worked remains much in its old condition, with the table at which they sat, and some of their portraits on the wall. Everything here, in short, is interesting: the press-room, which was used almost continuously and practically without change—two of the antiquated presses of Plantin's own time remain—for nearly three centuries; the Great and Little Libraries, with their splendid collection of books; the archive room, with its long series of business accounts and ledgers; the private livingrooms of the Moretus family; and last, but not least, the modest little shop, where books still repose upon the shelves, which looks as though the salesman might return at any moment to his place behind the counter. England has certainly nothing like it, though London had till recently in Crosby Hall a great merchant's house of the fifteenth century, though stripped of all internal fittings and propriety. Luckily this last has been re-erected at Chelsea, though robbed by the change of site of half its authenticity and value.

I have chosen to dwell on this strange museum at length that seems disproportionate, not merely because of its unique character, but because it seems to me full of lessons and reproach for an age that has subordinated honest workmanship to cheap and shoddy productiveness, and has sacrificed the workman to machinery. Certainly no one who visits Antwerp can afford to overlook it; but probably most people will first bend their steps towards the more popular shrine of the great cathedral. Here I confess myself utter heretic: to call this church, as I have seen it called, "one of the grandest in Europe," seems to me pure Philistinism—the cult of the merely big and obvious, to the disregard of delicacy and beauty. Big it is assuredly, and superficially astonishing; but anything more barn-like architecturally, or spiritually unexalting, I can hardly call to memory. Outside it lacks entirely all shadow of homogeneity; the absence of a central tower, felt perhaps even in the great cathedrals of Picardy and the Ile de France, just as it is felt in Westminster and in Beverley Minster, is here actually accentuated by the hideous little cupola—I hardly know how properly to call it—that squats, as though in derision, above the crossing; whilst even the natural meeting and intersection at this point of high roofs, which in itself would rise to dignity, is wantonly neglected to make way for this monstrosity. The church, in fact, looks, when viewed externally, more like four separate churches than one; and when we step inside, with all the best will in the world to make the best of it, it is hard to find, much to admire, and anything at all to love, in these acres of dismally whitewashed walls, and long, feeble lines of arcades without capitals. The inherent vice of Belgian architecture—its lack of really beautiful detail, and its fussy superfluity of pinnacle and panelling—seems to me here to culminate. Belgium has really beautiful churches—not merely of the thirteenth century, when building was lovely everywhere, but later buildings, like Mons, and St. Pierre at Louvain; but Antwerp is not of this category. Architecturally, perhaps, the best feature of the whole church is the lofty spire (over four hundred feet), which curiously resembles in general outline that of the Hotel de Ville at Brussels (three hundred and seventy feet), and dates from about the same period (roughly the middle of the fifteenth century). As usual in Belgium, it is quite out of scale; it is lucky, indeed, that the corresponding south-west tower has never been completed, for the combination of the two would be almost overwhelming. It is curious and interesting as an example of a tower tapering upwards to a point in a succession of diminishing stages, in contrast with tower and spire. France has something like it, though far more beautiful, in the thirteenth-century tower at Senlis; but England affords no parallel. I am not sure who invented the quite happy phrase, "Confectioner's Gothic," but this tower at Antwerp is not badly described by it. It is altogether too elaborate and florid, like the sugar pinnacle of a wedding-cake.

This cathedral of Antwerp, however, though at the time that it was built a mere collegiate church of secular canons, and only first exalted to cathedral rank in 1559, is one of the largest churches in superficial area in the world, a result largely due to its possession, uniquely, of not less than six aisles, giving it a total breadth of one hundred and seventy feet. Hung in the two transepts respectively are the two great pictures by Rubens—the "Elevation of the Cross" and the "Descent from the Cross"—that are described at such length, and with so much critical enthusiasm, by Sir Joshua Reynolds in his "Journey to Flanders and Holland." The "Descent from the Cross," painted by Rubens in 1612, when he was only thirty-five years old, is perhaps the more splendid, and is specially remarkable for the daring with which the artist has successfully ventured (what "none but great colourists can venture") "to paint pure white linen near flesh." His Christ, continues Sir Joshua, "I consider as one of the finest figures that ever was invented: it is most correctly drawn, and I apprehend in an attitude of the utmost difficulty to execute. The hanging of the head on His shoulder, and the falling of the body on one side, gives such an appearance of the heaviness of death, that nothing can exceed it." Antwerp, of course, is full of magnificent paintings by Rubens, though unfortunately the house in which he lived in the Place de Meir (which is traversed by the tram on its way from the Est Station to the Place Verte), which was built by him in 1611, and in which he died in 1640, was almost entirely rebuilt in 1703. There is another great Crucifixion by the master in the Picture Gallery, or Palais des Beaux Arts, which illustrates his exceptional power as well as his occasional brutality." The centurion, with his hands on the nape of his horse's neck, is gazing with horror at the writhings of the impenitent thief, whose legs are being broken with an iron bar, which has so tortured the unhappy man that in his agony he has torn his left foot from the nail." It is questionable whether any splendour of success can ever justify a man in thus condescending to draw inspiration from the torture-room or shambles.

One would gladly spend more time in this Antwerp gallery, which exceeds, I think, in general magnificence the collections at Brussels and Amsterdam; and gladly would one visit the great fifteenth and sixteenth century churches of St. Jacques, St. Andre, and St. Paul, which not merely form together architecturally an important group of a strongly localized character, but are also, like the cathedral, veritable museums or picture galleries. It is necessary, however, to conclude this section, to say a few words about Louvain, which, lying as it does on the main route from Brussels to Liege, may naturally be considered on our way to the northern Ardennes.

Louvain, on the whole, has been much more modernized than other Belgian cities of corresponding bulk, such as Bruges or Malines. The road from the railway-station to the centre of the town is commonplace indeed in its lack of picturesque Flemish house-fronts or stepped, "corbie," Flemish gables. Louvain, in fact, unlike the two "dead" cities of West Flanders and Brabant, wears a briskly business-like aspect, and pulses with modern life. I suppose that I ought properly to have written all this in the past tense, for Louvain is now a heap of smoking cinders. The famous Town Hall has, indeed, so far been spared by ruffians who would better have spared the magnificent Cloth Hall at Ypres; between these two great buildings, the products respectively of the Belgian genius of the fifteenth and thirteenth centuries, "culture" could hardly hesitate. The Hotel-de-Ville at Louvain is, indeed, an astonishing structure, just as the cathedral at Antwerp is astonishing; but one has to be very indulgent, or very forgetful of better models, not to deprecate this absolutely wanton riot of overladened panelling and bulging, top-heavy pinnacles. The expiring throes of Belgian Gothic were a thousand degrees less chaste than the classicism of the early Renaissance: few, perhaps, will prefer the lacelike over-richness of this midfifteenth century town hall at Louvain to the restraint of the charming sixteenth-century facade of the Hotel de Ville at Leiden. Opposite the town hall is the huge fifteenth-century church of St. Pierre, the interior of which, still smothered in whitewash in 1910, was remarkable for its florid Gothic rood-screen and soaring Tabernacle, or Ciborium. The stumpy fragment of tower at the west end is said once to have been five hundred and thirty feet high! It is not surprising to read that this last, and crowning, manifestation of a familiar Belgian weakness was largely wrecked by a hurricane in 1604.

CHAPTER IV

One has left oneself all too little space to say what ought to be said of the Belgian Ardennes. Personally I find them a trifle disappointing; they come, no doubt, as a welcome relief after the rest of Belgian landscape, which I have heard described, not altogether unjustly, as the ugliest in the world; but the true glory and value of Belgium will always be discovered in its marvellously picturesque old towns, and in its unrivalled wealth of painting, brass-work, and wood-carving. Compared with these last splendours the low, wooded wolds of the Ardennes, with their narrow limestone valleys, seem a little thing indeed. Dinant, no doubt, and Rochefort would be pleasant places enough if one were not always harking back in memory to Malines and Ypres, or longing to be once more in Ghent or Bruges.

The traveller by railway between Brussels and Liege passes, soon after leaving the station of Ans, a point of great significance in the study of Belgian landscape. Hitherto from Brussels, or for that matter from Bruges and Ostend, the country, though studded at frequent intervals with cities and big towns, has been curiously and intensely rural in the tracts that lie between; but now, as we descend the steep incline into the valley of the Meuse, we enter on a scene of industrial activity which, if never quite as bad as our own Black Country at home, is sufficiently spoilt and irritating to all who love rustic grace. The redeeming point, as always, is that infinitely superior good taste which presents us, in the midst of coal-mines and desolation, not with our own unspeakably squalid Sheffields or Rotherhams, but with a queenly city, with broad and handsome streets, with a wealth of public gardens, and with many stately remnants of the Renaissance and Middle Time. It is possible in Liege to forget—or rather impossible to recall—the soiled and grimy country that stretches from its gates in the direction of Seraing. Even under the sway of the Spanish tyranny this was an independent state under the rule of a Bishop Prince, who was also an Elector of the Holy Roman Empire. Its original cathedral, indeed, has vanished, like those at Cambrai and Bruges, in the insensate throes of the French Revolution; and the existing church of St. Paul, though dating in part from the thirteenth century, and a fine enough building in its way, is hardly the kind of structure that one would wish to associate with the seat of a bishopric that is still so historic, and was formerly so important and even quasi-regal. Here, however, you should notice, just as in the great neighbour church of St. Jacques, the remarkable arabesque-pattern painting of the severies of the vault, and the splendour of the sixteenth-century glass. St. Jacques, I think, on the whole is the finer church of the two, and remarkable for the florid ornament of its spandrels, and for the elaborate, pendent cusping of the soffits of its arches—features that lend it an almost barbaric magnificence that reminds one of Rosslyn Chapel. Liege, built as it is exactly on the edge of the Ardennes, is far the most finely situated of any great city in Belgium. To appreciate this properly you should not fail to climb the long flight of steps—in effect they seem interminable, but they are really about six hundred—that mounts endlessly from near the Cellular Prison to a point by the side of the Citadelle Pierreuse. Looking down hence on the city, especially under certain atmospheric conditions—I am thinking of a showery day at Easter—one is reminded of the lines by poor John Davidson:

> "The adventurous sun took Heaven by storm;
> Clouds scattered largesses of rain;
> The sounding cities, rich and warm,
> Smouldered and glittered in the plain."

It is not often that one is privileged to look down so directly, and from so commanding a natural height, on to so vast and busy a city—those who like this kind of comparison have styled it the Belgian Birmingham—lying unrolled so immediately, like a map, beneath our feet.

From Liege, if you like, you may penetrate the Ardennes—I do not know whether Shakespeare was thinking in "As You Like It" of this woodland or of his own Warwickshire forest of Arden; perhaps he thought of both—immediately by way of Spa and the valley of the Vesdre, or by the valleys of the Ourthe and of its tributary the Ambleve; or you may still cling for a little while to the fringe of the Ardennes, which is also the fringe of the industrial country, and explore the valley of the Meuse westward, past Huy and Namur, to Dinant. Huy has a noble collegiate church of Notre Dame, the chancel towers of which (found again as far away as Como) are suggestive of Rhenish influence, but strikes one as rather dusty and untidy in itself. Namur, on the contrary, we have already noted with praise, though it has nothing of real antiquity. The valley of the Meuse is graced everywhere at intervals with fantastic piles of limestone cliff, and certainly, in a proper light, is pretty; but there is far too much quarrying and industrialism between Liege and Namur, and far too many residential villas along the banks between Namur and Dinant, altogether to satisfy those who have high ideals of scenery. Wordsworth, in a prefatory note to a sonnet that was written in 1820, and at a date when these signs of industrialism were doubtless less obtrusive, says: "The scenery on the Meuse pleases one more, upon the whole, than that of the Rhine, though the river itself is much inferior in grandeur"; but even he complains that the scenery is "in several places disfigured by quarries, whence stones were taken for the new fortifications." Dinant, in particular, has an exceptionally grand cliff; but the summit is crowned (or was) by an ugly citadel, and the base is thickly clustered round with houses (not all, by any means, mediaeval and beautiful) in a way that calls to mind the High Tor at Matlock Bath. Dinant, in short, is a kind of Belgian Matlock, and appeals as little as Matlock to the "careful student" of Nature. If at Dinant, however, you desert the broad valley of the Meuse for the narrow and secluded limestone glen of the Lesse, with its clear and sparkling stream, you will sample at once a kind of scenery that reminds you of what is best in Derbyshire, and is also best and most characteristic in the Belgian Ardennes. The walk up the stream from Dinant to Houyet, where the valley of the Lesse becomes more open and less striking, is mostly made by footpath; and the pellucid river is crossed, and recrossed, and crossed again, by a constant succession of ferries. Sometimes the white cliff rises directly from the water, sheer and majestic, like that which is crowned by the romantic Chateau Walzin; sometimes it is more broken, and rises amidst trees from a broad plinth of emerald meadow that is interposed between its base and the windings of the river. Sometimes we thread the exact margin of the stream, or traverse in the open a scrap of level pasture; sometimes we clamber steeply by a stony path along the sides of an abrupt and densely wooded hillside, where the thicket is yellow in spring with Anemone Ranunculoides, or starred with green Herb Paris. This is the kind of glen scenery that is found along the courses of the Semois, Lesse, and Ourthe, recalling, with obvious differences, that of Monsal Dale or Dovedale, but always, perhaps, without that subtle note of wildness that robes even the mild splendours of Derbyshire with a suggestion of mountain dignity. The Ardennes, in short—and this is their scenic weakness—never attain to the proper mountain spirit. There is a further point, however, in which they also recall Derbyshire, but in which they are far preeminent. This is the vast agglomeration of caves and vertical potholes—like those in Craven, but here called etonnoirs—that riddle the rolling wolds in all directions. Chief among these is the mammoth cave of Han, the mere perambulation of which is said to occupy more than two hours. I have never penetrated myself into its sombre and dank recesses, but something may be realized of its character and scale merely by visiting its gaping mouth at Eprave. This is the exit of the Lesse, which, higher up the vale, at the curious Perte de Lesse, swerves suddenly from its obvious course, down the bright and cheerful valley, to plunge noisily through a narrow slit in the rock—

> "Where Alph, the sacred river, ran
> Through caverns measureless to man
> Down to a sunless sea."

Rochefort, which itself has a considerable cave, is a pleasant centre for the exploration of these subterranean marvels. Altogether this limestone region of the Ardennes, though certainly not remarkable for mountain or forest splendour, comes as a somewhat welcome relief after the interminable levels and chessboard fields of East and West Flanders, or of the provinces of Limburgh and Antwerp.

Note:

Note: